Mighty Machines

Garbage Trucks

by Terri DeGezelle

Consulting Editor: Gail Saunders-Smith, PhD

Consultant: Alice Jacobsohn
Director, Public Affairs and Industry Research
National Solid Wastes Management Association
Washington, DC

Capstone
press

Mankato, Minnesota

Pebble Plus is published by Capstone Press,
151 Good Counsel Drive, P.O. Box 669, Mankato, Minnesota 56002.
www.capstonepress.com

1 2 3 4 5 6 11 10 09 08 07 06

Library of Congress Cataloging-in-Publication Data
DeGezelle, Terri, 1955–
    Garbage trucks / by Terri DeGezelle.
    p. cm.—(Pebble plus. Mighty machines)
    Summary: "Simple text and photographs present garbage trucks, their parts, and their jobs"—Provided by
publisher.
    Includes bibliographical references and index.
    ISBN-13: 978-0-7368-5356-9 (hardcover)
    ISBN-10: 0-7368-5356-1 (hardcover)
    1. Refuse collection vehicles—Juvenile literature. 2. Refuse and refuse disposal—Juvenile literature.
I. Title. II. Series.
TD794.D4285 2006
629.225—dc22   2005021605

Editorial Credits
Martha E. H. Rustad, editor; Molly Nei, set designer; Ted Williams, book designer;
    Wanda Winch, photo researcher; Scott Thoms, photo editor

Photo Credits
Capstone Press/Karon Dubke, cover, 7, 9, 11, 13, 15, 21; Corbis/Sygma/Next Photo/Kwok Wing Kuen, 19;
Index Stock Imagery/Elfi Kluck, 17; Index Stock Imagery/Omni Photo Communications Inc., 5; iStockphoto/
Niilo Tippler, 1

The author thanks Mark Hibbs, Engineer, Heil Company, for his assistance with this book.
Pebble Plus thanks Waste Management of Mankato, Minnesota for assistance with photo shoots.

Note to Parents and Teachers

The Mighty Machines set supports national standards related to science, technology, and society. This book describes and illustrates garbage trucks. The images support early readers in understanding the text. The repetition of words and phrases helps early readers learn new words. This book also introduces early readers to subject-specific vocabulary words, which are defined in the Glossary section. Early readers may need assistance to read some words and to use the Table of Contents, Glossary, Read More, Internet Sites, and Index sections of the book.

Table of Contents

A Garbage Truck's Job

A garbage truck picks up
and dumps garbage.

Garbage Truck Parts

Garbage trucks have
lights that flash.
The lights warn people
to stay out of the way.

lights

101645

WM
WASTE MANAGEMENT

⚠ **CAUTION**
VEHICLE STOPS AND BACKS FREQUENTLY

CAUTION
WIDE
RIGHT
TURNS
DO NOT PASS
ON RIGHT

MINNESOTA
YA P3408P
10,000 LAKES

WM
WASTE MANAGEMENT

WM
WASTE MANAGEMENT

STOP

Garbage trucks have arms
that pick up garbage cans.
The arms dump the garbage
into the hopper.

hopper

arm

Garbage trucks have packing panels. Packing panels crush the garbage in the hopper.

packing panel

Garbage truck drivers

sit inside the cab.

They push buttons to move

the arm and packing panel.

A screen shows drivers
the inside of the hopper.
The screen also helps drivers
back up safely.

screen

What Garbage Trucks Do

Garbage trucks pick up
garbage around town.
Some trucks pick up items
for recycling too.

Garbage trucks dump
garbage at landfills.
Newspapers, bottles,
and cans are taken
to recycling centers.

Mighty Garbage Trucks

Garbage trucks pick up,
carry, and dump garbage.
Garbage trucks are
mighty machines.

Glossary

flash—to blink on and off

hopper—a container on a garbage truck that holds garbage

landfill—a large area of land where garbage is buried

packing panel—a large, flat piece of metal that crushes garbage tightly in the hopper

recycling—remaking old items such as newspapers, glass bottles, or aluminum cans into new items

warn—to tell a person there may be danger

Read More

Bridges, Sarah. *I Drive a Garbage Truck.* Working Wheels. Minneapolis: Picture Window Books, 2004.

Fontes, Justine. *Trash.* Matchbox Books. Middleton, Wis.: Pleasant Company, 2002.

LeBoutillier, Nate. *A Day in the Life of a Garbage Collector.* First Facts: Community Helpers at Work. Mankato, Minn.: Capstone Press, 2005.

Internet Sites

FactHound offers a safe, fun way to find Internet sites related to this book. All of the sites on FactHound have been researched by our staff.

Here's how:

1. Visit *www.facthound.com*

2. Type in this special code **0736853561** for age-appropriate sites. Or enter a search word related to this book for a more general search.

3. Click on the **Fetch It** button.

FactHound will fetch the best sites for you!

Index

Word Count: 131
Grade: 1
Early-Intervention Level: 16